Dear Parents,

Thank you for purchasing our book. We are thrilled to be part of your child's reading journey. By choosing this book, you have taken an important first step in improving your child's reading skills.

To make the most out of this book, we recommend reading one to two stories a day for about thirty minutes. Feel free to break this session into two parts if needed to keep your child engaged and focused. After reading, encourage your child to color the picture that accompanies each story. This not only makes learning fun but also reinforces what they have just read.

We understand that starting a new reading program can feel overwhelming, but remember that consistency is key. Setting aside dedicated reading time each day will help build a strong routine and foster a love for reading in your child. If you're unsure where to start, focusing on vowel sounds in order we have provided is a great approach. This foundational skill is crucial for developing strong reading abilities and will give your child the confidence they need to progress.

Additionally, creating a comfortable and distraction-free reading environment can make a significant difference. Choose a quiet spot where your child can concentrate, and make sure they have all the materials they need, including crayons for coloring. Positive reinforcement and praise can also motivate your child and make the learning experience enjoyable.

Should you need any guidance or a FREE placement test, please don't hesitate to reach out. We are here to support you and your child every step of the way. Our goal is to provide you with the tools and resources necessary to make reading a positive and rewarding experience.

Thank you once again for your support. Together, we can make a significant difference in your child's reading journey. Your commitment and involvement play a crucial role in their success, and we are honored to be a part of this important milestone.

Warm regards,
Budding Brains Books

TABLE OF CONTENTS

TABLE OF CONTENTS

Blend pr

Consonant Blends
Bl

Blu the bug had a big, blue blob. Blu and the blue blob had fun. Blu slid on the blob. The blob was slick! Blu slid and slid. Blu did not slip! Blu and the blob had a blast. Blu said, "Blue blobs are the best!" Blu and the blob then sat in the sun.

Blair the goat loves to bleat. One day, Blair spots a big blue blot on the barn wall. He blinks and bleats loud. "Blip, blip," goes Blair, glad at the blue blob. It's just a blob, but Blair keeps on with his bleats, glad and bold. Each bleat is big and fills the farm with fun. Blair's bleat is the best!

Bill likes to play ball. He gets a big blush on his face when he plays with his black pants. Bill will toss the ball and then blink. He blinks as he blushes with a bluff. Bill's pals clap and yell, "Bill is the best!" Bill grins and his blush is bright. Bill feels glad as he plays with his pals. They all play till dusk.

Blu the bug had a big blue block. Blu slid the block to the top of the hill. The block slid down fast and hit a black log. Blu did not sob. He got the block and slid it up again. The block slid down and hit a blank bell. The bell rang loud. Blu was glad.

Bliss the bug had a big day. He saw a big bloom by a blue bell. Bliss sat on the blank bloom and sang a glad song. The bloom was his best spot to rest. Bliss had lots of fun in the sun. With a blip, Bliss was blessed.

Blip the blob had a bland plan. He slid past a plug and a plum. Blip met a blue bird by a blip on a map. The bird sang a bland song. Blip and the bird then put a blot of ink on a bland blog. They had lots of fun and blast off in the blessed sun.

Consonant Blend

Cl

Clad the clam was sad. He sat on a rock and did not clap or clack. Clad had no clan to chat with. He saw a clip and got a plan. Clad had to be slick to grab it. He slid from the rock and hit the clip. Clad the clam had a clan tag now. He was glad.

Clack the clown has a big, red nose. He likes to clap and clap in his cool, blue pants. Clack's dog, Clip, can clap too. Clip claps along with Clack. They make all the kids clap and laugh. Clack gives Clip a clap and a pat. What a fun day at the play!

Clif the cloud was up in the sky. He was a big, classy cloud . Clif was full of rain. One day, Clif let the rain clamp, clash, and clap on the cliffs. The cliffs had been dry. The rain made all the cliffs wet. Clif was glad to help. The cliffs had a lot of fun in the wet day. Clif felt glad.

Clay has a big clock. The clock sits on a class wall. The clock ticks and tocks. It is time to clap and play! Clay claps and runs to the clock. He climbs up and looks at it. "Tick, tock," says the clock. Clay is glad. It is fun to hear the clock clash and click!

Clam had a clip. Clam put the clip on a club map. The map fell. Clam got a plan. He put the clip on a cloth flag. The clip slid and the cloth flag fell. Clam then put the clip on a clutch bill. The bill did not fall. Clam was glad

Cleo has a blue cloth. She lets the cloth drop. The cloth hits a clump of mud. Cleo claps. She cleans the mud off the cloth. Cleo clips the cloth on a line. A gust of wind clips the cloth. The cloth flaps and then it is still. Cleo is glad. Her blue cloth is clean and dry.

Consonant Blend

Fl

Flap the fly has a plan. He will flip and flap from plant to flag. Flap flies to a flat spot and flits up. He sees a floppy flag. Flap is glad he can fly fast to the flag. He flaps back and sits. Flap is a fun fly.

A flea fled from a flag on a flat log. Flo, the flea, flew fast to flip off the flag. She flops on a flip flop. Flo then flits to a plum and sips a flab of jam. Flo has fun and flaps off to nap on a soft fluff. Flo is glad and snug in the fluff.

Flap got a fluke at the flag fest. He flew to a flat spot and flung the flag. It flew off fast! Flap felt glad. He and Flop, his pal, did a flip. Then they fled to flop in a flap tent. What fun! They felt a flap gust. The flag flew back. What luck! Flap got the flag.

Flom the flame is small. Flom can flip and fly. One day, Flom was on a flat rock. A big wind came. It made Flom flap a lot. Flom did not flee. She felt the wind and flew high. Flom can glow and be bright. Now, Flom is not just a small flame. She is a big, bold flame.

Flap has a plan. A flake fell from the sky. Flap and Flop find the flake. It is flat. They flip the flake on a sled. They fling the flake, and it flies. Flap and Flop clap. The flake lands in a pond. Flop and Flap go flop on the sled. They flag a pal. "Let's play," Flap yells. They all sled till dusk.

Consonant Blend
Gl

Glen has a big glass globe. Glen was glad the globe was full of glitz and glam. Glen can spin the glass globe and see lots of lands. He spots a flag on the globe and a tiny glow from a town. Glen grins as he maps his trip with a plan. He will go to lots of lands one day. Glen's glass globe spins and stops on a land with hills. Glen is glad.

Glyn had a glint in her eyes. Glyn grabs her pink gloss. With a flick, she glides the gloss onto her lips. "Glow, glow!" she sings, glad for the glam look. Each day, Glyn uses the gloss and feels gleeful. "Gloss is my jam!" she looks at the glass. "With gloss, I am a star!" Glyn grins and goes to play, her lips all aglow.

Glob has a big, blue glass. He fills the glass with cold milk. Glob sips the milk and grins. "Glad I got this glass," he says. Glob puts the glass on a slab. He pats his dog and then jogs off. A gust of wind flips the glass. Milk spills all over! Glob gets a mop and glumly cleans up.

Glum has a big glossy glove. The glove is glad to grip and grab Glum's hands. Glum and the glove go to the glitch glen. They glide on the sled and grab globs of sticks. Glum is glad glove is a big help in the cold. Glum and the glove go back home, glad for the fun day in the glitch glen. Glum gives the glove a good spot to rest.

Glen has glue. He puts the glue on an ugly glass. The glue is on the glass but Glen did not like it. Glen claps. He lets the glue set. Glen gets a clip and a clam that glints in the sun. He adds glue to the clip. Glen is glad. The clip will hold the clam. The glue is good. Glen did a great job!

Glen the glum frog glid to the gloom of the glen. He had lost his glow. A glad glob of gold slid by. It glint with glee and gave Glen a grin. Glen grab it, and the glow was back! Now, glad, Glen glop and glid all day in the glen. The glow made him grin with glee. Glen's glum days were gone!

Consonant Blend
Pl

Plum and Flip spot a big plane. They plan to play in the plane. They plod to the plan. Flip taps the plane. The plane can zip up and up. It plows past a big pond. The plane is in the sky now! Plum and Flip clap and clap.

Plam had a small plan to play. She got a plot of land and a tiny plant. Plam dug a pit, put the plant in, and pats the soil flat. Each day, Plam plus pals look. They pull up bad plants and bugs. Soon, the plant is big and has buds. Plam and pals clap and plan a fun day to pick plums.

Pam had a blue plate plus plant food. Pam planned to put a plum on the plate. Pam had the plum and felt glad. Pam then plucked a clam on the plate. Pam ate the clam. Pam put a plant on the plate. Pam did not eat the plant. Pam just had fun.

Plum and Plod spot a plank. Plum taps the plank. Plod taps it, too. The plank flips! Plum and Plod grin. They plan to play on the plank. Plum sits, Plod jumps. The plank tips! What fun!

Plip the plug has a big job. He sits snug in the tub to stop the drip. When you plan a bath, drop him in the tub. Plip will plug the gap so the tub can fill up. With Plip in place, no drip will pass. He is a top plug for your tub! What is Plip?

Plum the plump plum sat on a flat plot of land. Plum was not glad, as he felt too bland. One day, a kid picked Plum up with a plan. "I will put Plum in a plum jam!" Plum got a zap of glee, as he knew he'd be a top plum jam in the land!

Consonant Blend Sl

Slim the slug slid slow on the slick slimy slot. Slim slept snug in the slot all day. Slim slid out at dusk to sip sap from a slab. Slim saw a slop and slid past fast. The slop was too grim for Slim. Slim slid back to the slot, snug and safe, and slept till dawn. Slim's life was slow but nice.

Sly slaps slimy slime on a slab. Sly slips on the slick slime. Sly slides, then stops. Sly slops the slime, slow and slick. Sly is glad. No more slides on slime!

Slip the sloth slid slow on the slim slick log. Slip slid past slim slugs and slosh in the slog. Slip slid to a slow stop. "Slog on, slog slow," Slip told the slugs. Slip slid on. Slip saw the slow sun set. Slip's slow slid was done. Slip slept snug.

Slam went to the door, and
Slim slid a slice of plum pie
onto a sled. "Plop!" went the
pie as it slid off. Slim slid on
the sled to grab the slice. "Sly!"
said Slim, as he got the slice
back. Now, Slim can snack!

Sam likes to sleep. Sam slips into his bed. The bed is snug. He slides into a soft slumber. A slow hum lulls Sam as he sleeps. Sam smiles in his sleep. The sun slinks up. Sam is still snug in his bed. He is glad to sleep late.

Slim and Slat slid on the slab. Slim slips and Slat slaps his lap. They slam and play. Slim and Slat have a blast on the slick slab. Slim grabs a sled. They slide fast. The slab is fun!

Consonant Blend

Br

Brit has big, brown braids. She grabs her bright red brush to groom her braids. She brags to Brad, her big bro, about her braids. Brad grins and gives Brit a big, blue ribbon. Brit puts the ribbon in her braids and grins back at Brad. Brit and Brad then grab bread and jam for a snack.

Brad has a big job. He bakes bread. Brad gets Bran and brand eggs to mix in a brass bin. He stirs the bran and brand eggs with a big grin. The mix will turn into a bran brand bun. Brad's bran brand bun is the best! Brad brags that his bran bun will win. Brad puts the bun in the oven. The bun is now done!

Brad the frog has a big, brass brick. Brad brushes the brick by a brook. Brad hops back and forth, from the brass brick to a branch. Brad grins and hops on the brick as he brags. Brad sits on the brick by the branch. Brad is glad with his brick by the brook.

Brad has a big brow. Brad's brow is so big that it can trap a lot of bran. Brad brags about his big, dry brow when it rains bran. He brims with glee. "Bring it on, rain!" Brad brays. Brad's brow is his brag. Brad is a brow king. Brad grins as his big brow brims with rain. Brad wins with his big brow.

Brit the frog likes to brag a lot. Brit bragged that she was the best at big jumps on a branch. One brisk day, Brit saw a big branch and bragged, "I bet I can jump that!" Brit took a big breath, ran fast, and then — brag! — she jumped. Brit's big brag was true; she did jump the big log. Brit felt proud.

Consonant Blend
Cr

Crisp air fills the day as Crow sits on a tree cross. He spots a crop not far off and crows with joy. With a crack and a crash, Crow is off. He grabs the crop, crunching it with glee. Crow then rests on the tree, proud and full from his find. Crow had a cry like a critic and set, waiting for his next crop.

Crab crept from the crib. Crab crawls past a crop and a crew. The crew digs and drops dirt. Crab clips on to a croc. The croc snaps! Crab slips and dips into a crack. Safe at last!

Cris has a crib. Cris can nap in the craft crib. The crib is big and did not crush Cris. A cat can nap in the crib too. Cris and the cat nap. The crib has a crisp mat. Cris can rub the cat. The cat can pur. They sit and nap. Cris and the cat nap in the crib.

Cruz has a big, red crown. The crown sits on a crusty box. Cruz can spin the crisp crown and it will not fall across the room. Cruz grins as the crown spins. The crown is not just fun, it is not crap. Cruz taps the crown and it stops. Now, Cruz will put the crown in the crusty box. Cruz is glad to have the crown.

Crab and Crow are pals. Crow spots a crop. It is crisp corn. Corn is a crop that Crab and Crow can peck to get crumbs. Crab and Crow grab at the corn. The crop of corn is big. Crab and Crow peck and peck. They crack the corn and grin. The crop of corn is now crumbs. The crop is fun. Crow and Crab nap by the crumbs.

Consonant Blend

Dr

Drew drops her red dress in the mud. She drips a lot of suds on the dress. Drew rubs the suds in to scrub the dress. She then drops the dress in a tub of suds. The dress drips dry. Drew is glad to see the dress is now as good as new. Drew grins and twirls in her clean red dress.

Drab the drum sat in a dry room. Until, "drip, drip, drip!" The drink fell on the roof. The dry room was not dry anymore. Drab dreamt of drum rolls in the rain. Then, a drop fell on Drab! "Yes!" Drab said. More drips drummed on his top. Drab's dream came to pass as he drummed along with the raindrops, filling the room with a drippy drama.

Drit had a drama for a dream. In the dream, Drit had a drill drum. He hit the drill drum and it made a loud drastic bump. A frog went to Drit. The frog did a drip, drop, draft dance to the drum. The frog was in a red dress and had a dry grin. Drit was glad in his dream.

Drab the drone drags a drop. Drab drops in a dry dock. Drab dips and drops. Drab drifts and drips. Drab drips on a drum. Drab drags the drum. Drab drops the drum. Drab drifts off.

Lila has a top pick for a drink. She will grin when she gets her drop and drip of the drink. It is not from a mix or a box. It is from a red cup. She will trim the tops and drop them in. Then she will drink a sip. Lila's best drink is a cup of fresh, cold, red fruit mix. She sips and her lips smack with joy!

Consonant Blend
Fr

Fred gets a fresh, frost fig. Fred grins, feeling frisky. He flips the fig from a frond, fast and free. The fig falls, Fred hops after. Fred grabs the frozen fig. "Fragrant!" Fred says. He flits off, full of glee. "Figs are fab!" Fred feels fine with his frosty find.

Fran sits by the fresh grill. She has a big bag of fries. Fran is frantic when she dips a fry in frothy red jam. She grins and eats it. Fran has fun with her fries. Fran Frolics. Fran is glad to have them. She will share with Brad. They both love fries.

Fred felt the frost from his front door, he saw frost on the frizzy tree. He frets, for his fresh figs may freeze. Fred grabs a frill from his flat and wraps the figs to fend off the frost. "Frost, go away!" Fred says with a grin. He frees the figs when the frost lifts. Fred's figs are fresh, free from frost's grip!

Frank had a big frown. Frank lost his frog in a frantic dash to confront bugs. Frank frets as he frisks for his frog. Frank's frown is deep as he finds no aspect of his pet. But then, a frill in the saffron frond! Frank grins as he sees his saffron frog hop from a frond. Happy, Frank gets him up. His frown flips to a fresh grin.

Consonant Blend Gr

Greg grabs a handful of grand grapes. Greg grins but the grape is grim. Greg grabs a pink grape. Greg grins and goes, "Mmm!" Greg's glad this grape is grand! Greg grabs more grapes. He gives some to Grock. Grock grins. "Great grapes!" Greg and Grock grin and eat the grand, pink grapes.

Greg and Gran go to a big, green grass plot. Gran lets Greg grab grass. Greg grins. Gran grins back. They grip the grass and play. The grass is grim with dirt. Greg and Gran drop the grass and go back

Grin has a big grill. Greg gets the grill hot and then grins. Grin puts fish and ribs on the grill. Greg grins as the fish and ribs sizz. The grill gets too hot! Greg grabs a rag to grab the ribs and fish. Greg and Grin grin and dig in. They chomp on the grub from the grill.

Grundy the hen had a grand plan. He saw a gram of grain in the barn. Greg went to grab the gram of grain, but he did not grasp it. The bag was grimy and Grundy slid and fell. But he did not give up. Grundy got up, gave a grin, and got the gram of grain. He had grit! Now Greg had gram of grain for his grub.

Greg, a groom, grabs a grey gift. He grins and grips it. The grand grid of green grins grows. Greg grins back. He gives the gift. Gram, the girl, grins and grabs the gift. Greg and Gram grab grub. They grin and sip grape grits. They grip hands and grin. Greg and Gram are glad.

Consonant Blend
Tr

Trent has a big red truck. The truck trips on a rock and drops a drum. Trent must fix the truck. He grabs a tool and tries to mend it. At last, the truck is all set. Trent and the truck trek to the park. They had fun in the sun.

Trug and Tris try to trap a tiny tree frog on the tracks. The train trips past. The frog trots off. Trug and Tris trot to track the frog. They trap the frog on a tray. "Tray trip for the frog!" grins Tris. The frog hops off. Trug grins. "Tricky frog!" he says. They trudge back to try again.

Travis has a red tray. He can put a lot of toys on the tray. Travis has a tiny toy. He puts the tiny toy on the tray too. Travis trips on a log. The tray tips and the toy drops. Travis is sad, but he can try to fix it. He sets the tray up and all is fine. Travis grins.

Trig and Tram trot to a big trash bin. Tram trips on a twig and yells, 'Trig, grab my hand!' Trig grabs him, and they drag a bag from the trash. In the bag, they find a trim map and a red tin. They grin and run back to trim the map's rim

Trex and Trix trot on a trail. They trek past a tree and a trim twig. Trex spots a trap. "Trip not," Trex tells Trix. Trix grins and steps past the trap. They trot on and find a trim tree fort. Trex and Trix grin and go in to rest.

Consonant Blend
Pr

A pro, Prum, had a plan to find a prop for a play. Prum swam past pink rock to grab the prop. Prum had a pep in his step. He saw a pram and felt it was just right. Prum took the pram to the play. The pro then put on a show with the pram. The pram was a hit at the play! It was like a press prank.

Pris had a present map. She put the map in a big print and pressed it as a proxy. The print was red. The print did not have a problem. Pris and Pam ran to see it. "A map print!" Pam said. "We can use it to find a pretty spot." Pris and Pam set the present print in the sun. They had fun with the map print.

Pris and the prism sat on a pretty mat. A bit of sun hit Pris and the prism like a prank. Red like bulbs lit up the wall from the prism like a proxy. Pris was so happy! A pro came to play and saw the prism. "Wow, Pris! How did you do that prism proxy?" Pris just spun and made bits of red. What fun! Pris and the pal had a top day with the prism.

Trug had a project prop. It was a prop frog. He set the prop on a prank log. Trug put the prop in an express spot. He ran to grab a bit of express props. Trug got a prop butterfly and a prop cap. He put all the props in a praxis box. "I love my props!" Trug said with a grin. Trug had no present problems.

FREE RESOURCES

If you want free resources,

please email

buddingbrainsbooksllc@gmail.com

to get access to our free

giveaways and strategy guides.

TEACHER GRATITUDE

Write a letter to a teacher who has had a memorable impact on your educational journey so far.

_____

_____

_____

_____

_____

_____

_____

_____

_____

Made in the USA
Las Vegas, NV
18 December 2024

14648267R00050